Extreme Sports

Rosalie Ajzensztejn

OXFORD
UNIVERSITY PRESS

OXFORD
UNIVERSITY PRESS

Great Clarendon Street, Oxford OX2 6DP

Oxford University Press is a department of the University of Oxford. It furthers the University's objective of excellence in research, scholarship, and education by publishing worldwide in

Oxford New York

Auckland Bangkok Buenos Aires Cape Town Chennai Dar es Salaam Delhi Hong Kong Istanbul Karachi Kolkata Kuala Lumpur Madrid Melbourne Mexico City Mumbai Nairobi São Paulo Shanghai Singapore Taipei Tokyo Toronto

with an associated company in Berlin

Oxford is a registered trade mark of Oxford University Press in the UK and in certain other countries

First published 2002

British Library Cataloguing in Publication Data

Data available

ISBN 0 19 917461 X

10 9 8 7 6 5 4 3 2 1

Also available in packs
Sports and Leisure Inspection Pack (one of each book) ISBN 0 19 917464 4
Extreme Sports Guided Reading Pack (six copies) ISBN 0 19 917869 0
Sports and Leisure Class Pack (six of each book) ISBN 0 19 917465 2

www.oup.com/uk/primary

Printed in Hong Kong

Acknowledgements

The Publisher would like to thank the following for their permission to reproduce photographs: p 1 Buzz Pictures; p 3 Buzz Pictures; p 4 Buzz Pictures; p 7 Corbis/Chris Trotman (top), Buzz Pictures (bottom); p 8 Buzz Pictures; p 10 Corbis/Lester V Bergman; p 11 Buzz Pictures; p 12 Buzz Pictures (both); p 14 Photoodisc/Chase Jarvis; p 15 Allsport USA/Mike Powell; p 16/17 Buzz Pictures (both); p 18 Buzz Pictures; p 19 Corbis/Douglas Peebles (top), Buzz Pictures (bottom); p 20 Buzz Pictures; p 21 Buzz Pictures; p 23 Buzz Pictures; p 24 Photoodisc/Karl Weatherly; p 25 Corbis; p 30 Mary Evans/Arthur Rackham Collection;

Front cover photograph by Photodisc/Karl Weatherly
Back cover by Buzz Pictures

Illustrated by David Russell and Martin Ursell

The publisher would like to thank the following advisers:
BERSA for their advice on Bungee Jumping; SSSprint for their advice on Street Luging;
Ding Boston of the Oxford Stunt Factory for his advice on these and other extreme sports.

Contents

Street Luging

Street luging is a high-speed dangerous sport that is performed on hills. It is well suited to the warm, dry climate and smooth, fast, hilly terrain of the streets of California. The official organization for street luging in the UK is SSSprint, founded in 1995. It runs the British Street Luging Competition. Street lugers are capable of speeds of 130 kph. It is now considered a competitive sport and features in the X-Games, in the USA, where extreme sports are presented in Olympic style.

▲ The luge is a long craft (up to 2.5 m long). The rider or "pilot" operates it from a lying-down position. The pilots steer by "leaning" from side to side, which shifts their weight slightly.

Gear for the pilot

The pilot wears a leather suit and a full-face motor-cycle helmet which is adapted to enable the rider to have good vision from his or her lying-down position.

The one-piece leather suit is fitted with extra padding in the seat and elbows, and a plastic pad is added to protect the spine. The pilot also wears thick leather gauntlets.

Equipment

A street luge (bought or made)

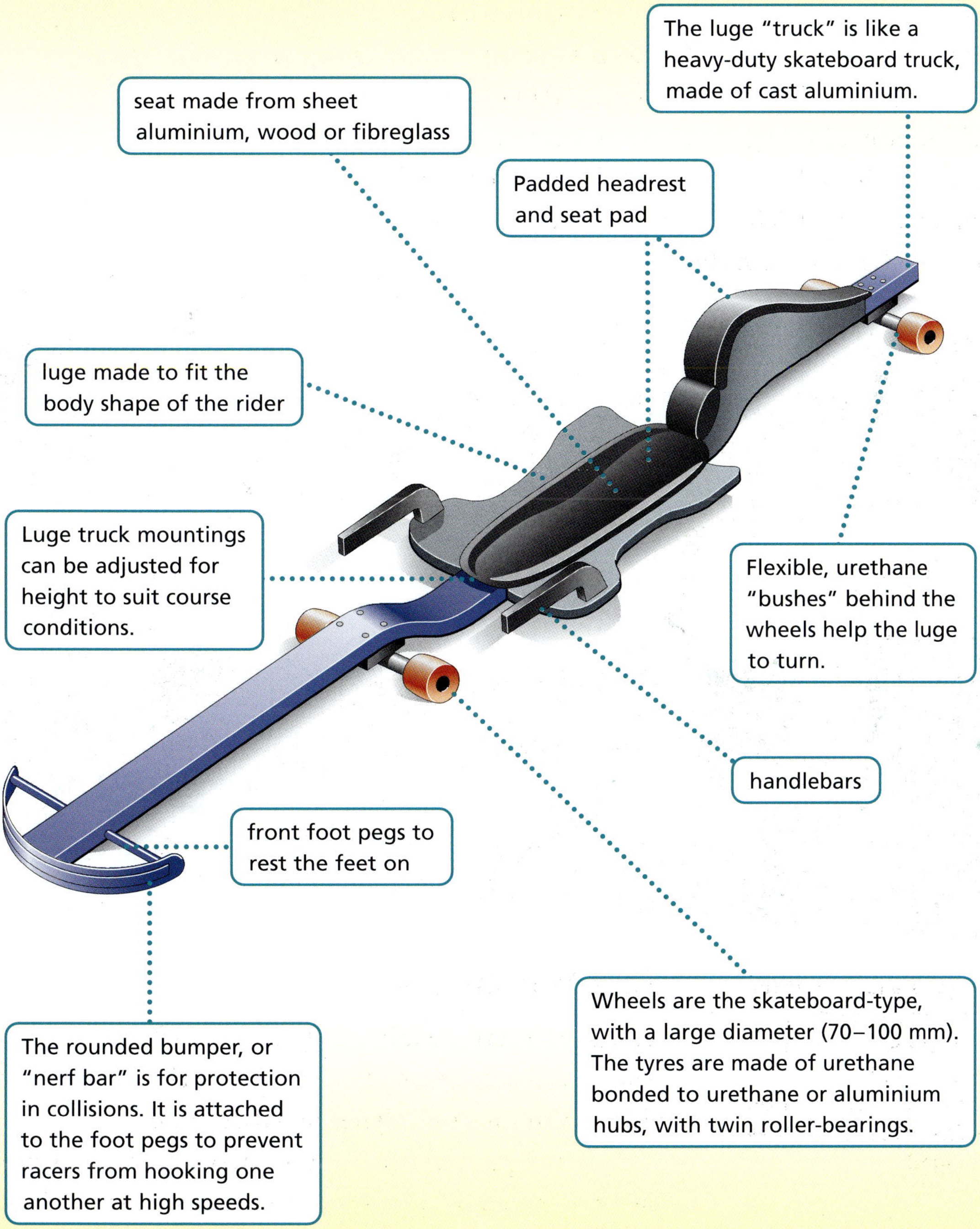

WHY DO IT?

Jim, a street luger from San Francisco

"Luging gives you such a thrill! The adrenaline rush is wicked!"

"But it's so dangerous!"

Josie, Jim's mother

"Street luging began on city streets, but the public are seriously afraid of the danger and see it as a cheap-thrill ride. Sure it can be dangerous, but I wear protective clothing so I don't get hurt badly if I crash. I get out of the way if anything comes behind me. I stay out of the way of people. Because it's illegal, we've been forced off the streets and into parking garages. It's so unfair that cyclists are allowed on the roads and street lugers are not."

The lingo

amped To be filled with the adrenaline rush that comes with street luging.

chucking bales Hitting the hay bales (which line the tracks as barriers) hard enough to move them.

drop a hill To ride a luge course.

flame Caused by luge wheels catching fire as a result of high speed.

flesh wing Extending an arm during a run for steering.

hysteria Uncontrolled wobble during a run.

junkyard Luges left on the track after a multiple collision.

▲ Street luging races have become extremely popular. They are held on streets closed to traffic, or on private roads. Street lugers can reach speeds of 130 kph.

▼ Lugers need thick soles on their boots because they brake with their feet.

Snowboarding

Snowboarding combines the grace of surfing with the spin and jump techniques of skateboarding.

Developed in the 1960s, snowboarding is believed to have started in the USA where people experimented with the idea of "surfing on the snow". The sport developed very quickly and the early basic boards changed as specialized designs were made to meet the demands of different competitions.

In 1994, snowboarding was declared an Olympic Sport.

Equipment

A board

The basic board is like a skateboard without wheels. The average-sized board is about 150 cm in length and 25 cm in width.

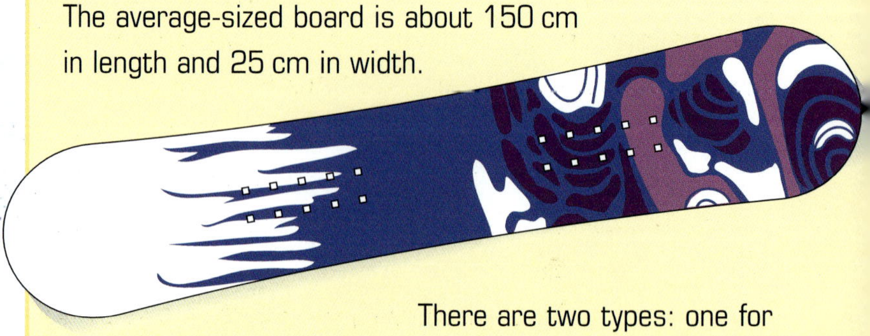

There are two types: one for freeriding downhill, the other for freestyle boarding, which includes "riding the pipe" and doing the jumps that make such good TV viewing.

HOW TO GET STARTED

- Strap your front foot onto the board. This places your toes over one edge and your heel against the other.
- Push off with your free back foot as if you were propelling a skateboard.

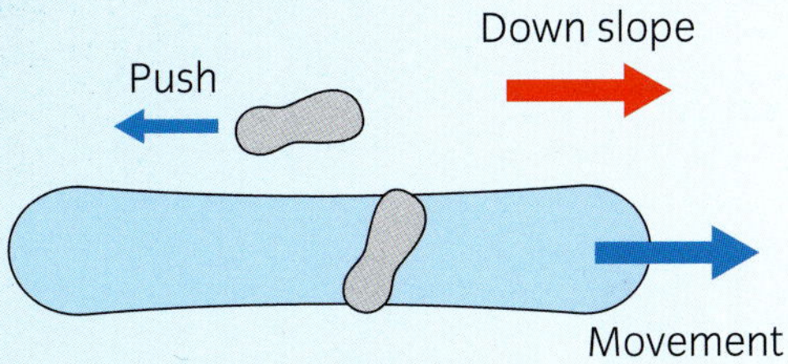

- Try not to catch the edge of the board too sharply in the snow as this will cause you to crash.
- To make a turn, lean forwards or backwards and from side to side, using the toe edge and the heel edge of the board for speed control.

- When you are ready to start going downhill, strap your back foot in and allow yourself to drift down the mountain.
- Face forwards, keeping your hands in front of you and your knees bent.
- To stop, turn until the board is across the slope, and skid to a stop.

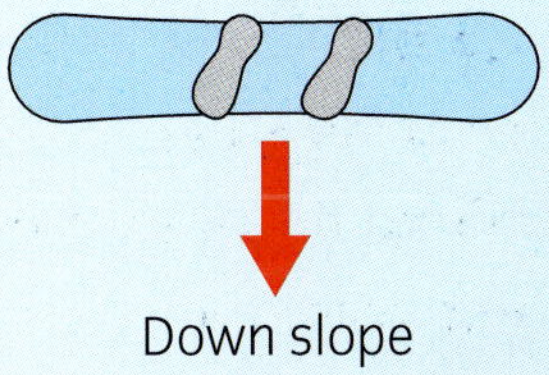

Bindings

Your boots are attached to the board with bindings. These have base plates and straps that can be tightened with a ratchet. Unlike ski bindings they are not meant to release when you crash. If you want to skate or glide along flat areas you have to disconnect one binding and push with the free foot.

For advanced boarders, the base plate is replaced with a set of rails which allow your foot to be in direct contact with the board. This gives a better feel and a faster response.

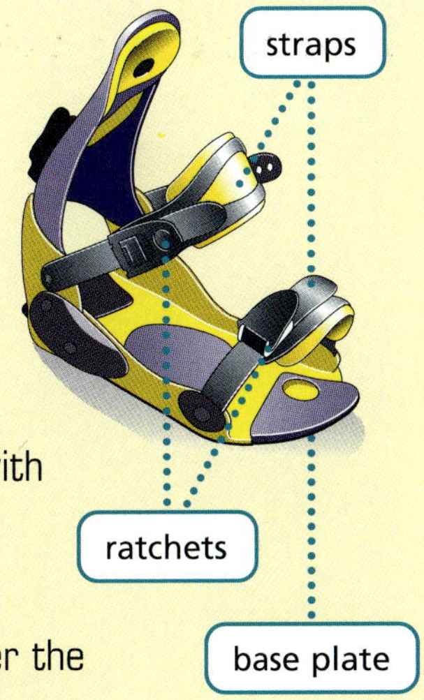

Boots

These are usually chunky, thick boots made in either the latest hi-tech materials or leather. They have rounded, blunt toes which make your feet look quite small. You will usually require one size larger than your normal shoes.

WHY DO IT?

"I started snowboarding when I was twelve-and-a-half. I saw this picture in a sports magazine and just knew that I had to do that."

James Jeffries, at 14, was the youngest member of the British Snowboard Team.

Dr Bill Smith is a specialist in sports injuries.

"Do you see many broken legs as a result of snowboarding?"

"I don't see that many. Upper limb injuries are more common. They are the result of falling onto an outstretched arm, so I see more wrist fractures than anything else. Methods are constantly being developed to reduce this risk. Many snowboarding injuries occur to people who have not bothered to have proper instruction, which is never a wise move."

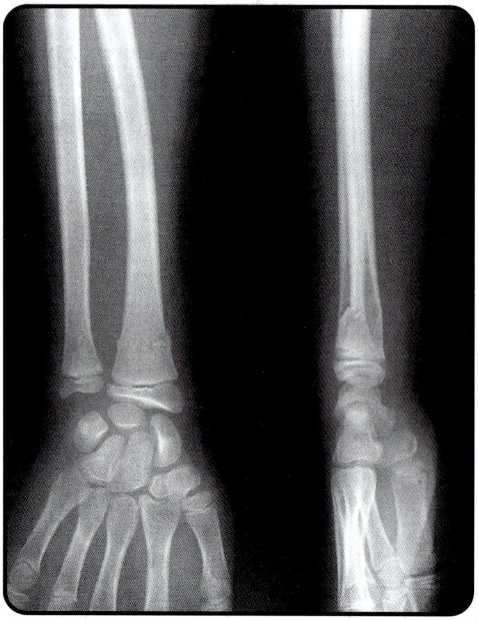

◀ Wrist fractures are the most common snowboarding injury.

The lingo

air Any aerial trick.

boned This describes the style element of a trick. The rider's arms or legs are stretched or straightened.

crail air The rear hand grabs the toe edge in front of the front foot while the rear leg is boned (stretched).

fakie Riding backwards.

halfpipe This is similar to a skateboard halfpipe. It is made of snow and is generally built on a slope. It is about 200 metres in length, of variable width and has a flat bottom which curves upwards to the vertical sides. Spins, flips and board grabs are performed in a halfpipe.

▲ Attempting a spin in a halfpipe

hucker A rider who throws himself or herself wildly through the air and does not land on his feet.

nose Front tip of the snowboard.

ollie Method of getting into the air without a jump by first lifting the front foot, then lifting the back foot as you spring off the tail.

rock and roll Boarder rides up a wall, balances on the top edge of a halfpipe and then re-enters the pipe smoothly without turning at all.

rolling down the windows When a rider is caught off balance and waves their arms in the air while trying to recover.

Aggressive Skating

Aggressive skating is not about aggression. The skating may be aggressive but the people doing it and the attitude are not. It is all about fun. It is skating for yourself and helping those around you to have a great time too. Skaters can reach terrific speeds, which makes this one of the most dangerous extreme sports. It is recognized as a competitive sport in the X-Games.

▲ The world-record speed for aggressive skating is over 100 kph.

In-line skates have a brake pad behind the wheels. ▶

Skating gear

Most skaters just wear a T-shirt and baggy jeans or trousers. A well-fitting helmet is an excellent safety precaution. Elbow and knee pads and fingerless leather gloves with wrist braces can be worn for extra protection.

Equipment

The skate boots

An expert should measure your feet to make sure the skate boots fit properly.

Sit down to have the length, arch and width of both feet measured, then stand up and note any changes. A noticeable change could mean that you tend to turn one or both feet inwards and you may need a specially made insole. Both feet should feel comfortable and snug in the skate boots.

The lining

Some boots come with a thin lining like a sock, others have thick, comfy liners inside. The lining should be well made and even throughout, with extra padding in the toes.

Lace-up liners offer greater support and fit better than the regular stitched liners.

The wheels

The ideal wheel shape is a wide wheel with a flat surface. This gives the largest and most stable base for tricks.

durometer: An instrument which measures hardness. Hard wheels are used to make them hard-wearing and to reduce grip for easier slides and **grinds**. The heavier you are, the harder the wheels have to be, so the wheels don't wear down too quickly. Softer wheels cushion the impact if you want to do jumps and stair rides.

core: Most aggressive skate wheels have small hard cores, or none at all. This keeps the wheels strong and tough enough to stand up to the pounding from street and **vert** skating.

Wheel setups

Standard flat
For jumps, stairs and ramps.

Anti-rocker
The main disadvantage of this setup is loss of stability. The skater loses some control and manoeuvring ability.

Large 65 mm outer wheels to give speed and smoothness

Tiny 45 mm middle wheels provide a larger grinding space.

Flat rocker
Combines speed of standard setup, grinding ability of small setup and stability of 55 mm outer wheels and 52 mm inner wheels. Middle wheels are rockered.

Stair-riding is a favourite stunt.

WAS IT WORTH IT?

Mrs Lawson is 50 years old. She is having a plaster cast put on her hand.

"How did that happen, Mrs Lawson?"

"It happened when I was aggressive skating."

Doctor

"Were you going fast?"

Mrs Lawson

"It's a bit embarrassing. You see, I wasn't moving at all. It's when you are standing still that it is difficult to balance."

The lingo

allez–oop A move in which you turn one way while rotating the other way.

armour Your pads – wear them with pride.

bunny A new skater who is always holding on to things for support.

bump Stair-riding, as in "let's go bump some stairs".

coping The metal bar going horizontally across the top of a ramp for easier grinding.

dropping in Doing a ramp when you enter it from the top.

grind Where you jump onto something and skid down it on the sides of your skates.

grommet A young skater.

late tricks A spinning trick done just before you land.

pump What you do to gain speed on ramps. It involves bending and extending your legs and pumping your arms to help you along.

vert A ramp that curves up to a vertical wall.

wax Scraping wax onto curbs or rails for easier grinding.

▲ Competitions can involve performing amazing spins, jumps and tricks.

Boogie Boarding

Boogie boarding is a water sport, often taken up as an introduction to surfing.

In Australia, many children are given their first boogie board at an early age, to use as a swimming aid, instead of a swimming ring or arm bands. Australians who spend a lot of time in the water become highly skilled in what can be an extremely dangerous sport.

Equipment

A boogie board

Compared to the cost of most sports equipment, boogie boards are relatively cheap.

The length of the board depends on your height. The taller the rider, the longer the board should be. It should come up to your belly button. If you ride smaller waves, the board can be a little longer, but if you ride big waves the board should be shorter.

The width of the nose influences the water displacement, speed and manoeuvrability of the board.

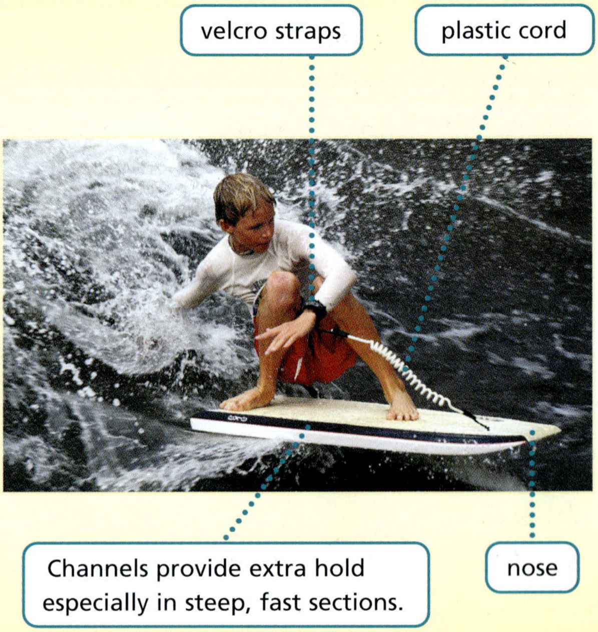

Boogie boarding is very dependent on the weather. It is possible to boogie board on low waves but the best waves are right before and after a storm. So winter is really the best time for boarding.

◀ It feels great when you "catch the wave".

Boogie boarding gear

Trunks or a bathing costume

Flippers or fins (optional)

A short bladed fin gives a quicker thrust motion. Fins are used to increase speed and make it easier to "catch the wave".

Fin tether cord to tie the fins to your feet.

Life jacket (especially if you are inexperienced)

Wetsuit for professional boarders or for those who want to board all year round. It must be skin-tight. It will help to keep you warm and will provide buoyancy, like a life jacket.

Maintenance

The top of the board should be waxed. Ensure the bottom of the board has no cuts as boogie boarding requires a smooth surface.

SO WHAT DO YOU DO?

- The idea of boogie boarding is to ride the waves.
- Lie down on your stomach on the board, kicking and holding on to it while riding a wave.
- The aim is to get up as high as you can on the face of the wave, stay in the wave and, as it crashes, you perform tricks and spins.
- When experienced, you can try riding the waves in an upright position and doing backflips.

Paddling

Wiping out

"Wiping out" means falling off your board while riding a wave. Know your limits and only ride the waves you feel ready for.

- Hold your breath.
- Stay calm and try not to fight the wave too hard.
- If you wipe out on a reef break, roll into a ball with your hands and arms over your head to protect your head from hitting the bottom.

Landing

Be aware of how deep or shallow the waves are breaking, as this will determine how you should land. If the waves are deep, dive deep and push through the back of the wave. If they are shallow and you are in an uncontrollable situation, spread your body out so that you make a shallower landing.

Don't fall on the shore side of your board if you can help it.

WHY DO IT?

"You must watch the water. When you come to a 'rapid' there is a drop of about a metre. When waves come up you see this steep drop. You go down and up and catch the wave. It feels great."

Dana, a boogie boarder

The lingo

backhand surfing Riding with one's back to the wave.

black holes A group of teenage kids who don't even go into the water.

Donald Duck A beginner trying to walk in his new fins – taking lots of falls.

double up Two waves that join.

snapped Getting hurt by a big wave.

sponge attack Splashing the boarder next to you by lifting a finned foot out of the water then back in quickly.

washing machine Being spun around under water a few times before being thrown up.

wet brain An uncoordinated boarder.

zooed out Crowded surf.

▼ Don't forget to hold your breath when you "wipe out".

Sport Climbing

Sport climbing is the most rapidly growing type of climbing. It has two advantages over traditional rock climbing: it is not as expensive, and more people are able to find somewhere to try it. You can sport climb on a wall or a rock, as well as on a mountain.

Cliffs are often used for sport climbing, which is fun and often competitive. The winner in a match would be the fastest or the best climber. In sport climbing you can complete many different routes in a single outing. It continues to draw new recruits all the time.

▲ Expert sport climbers need to be quick, light on their feet, and have good balance.

So what do you do?

Sport climbing can be done anywhere with fixed bolts or anchor points already in place – in gyms, on outdoor crags and on purpose-built walls designed for competition climbing. It involves high-intensity, difficult climbing on fairly short, pre-planned routes.

Climbers follow the route and clip their ropes into fixed bolts during their ascent. As the bolts and holds are already in place, the emphasis is on the physical skills involved in making the moves, rather than simply finding the route to the top.

Difficult moves are what count, so climbers don't waste time and energy carrying equipment or placing extra fixings for **protection**. The main aim is to be quick and light. Unlike in traditional climbing, falling is normal. You expect to fall while working out a difficult move. The climber's energy and time is spent on solving these moves.

Climbers are often attracted to indoor gyms with climbing walls because they offer a place to practise and train even in bad weather, or at night. The holds are changed frequently, so there are always new problems to attempt. Sport climbing standards are improving all the time.

We may see sport climbing as an Olympic sport in the future.

Equipment

rope
Hi-tech climbing rope, usually 9 or 11 mm thick, is strong but flexible and is made of nylon, or the new synthetic fibre, kevlar.

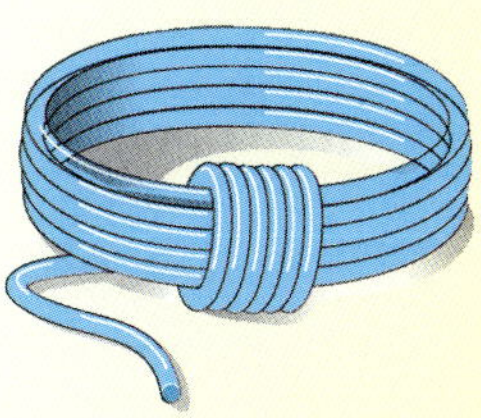

padded safety harnesses are light, streamlined and padded to cushion repeated falls. They are worn around the waist and thighs.

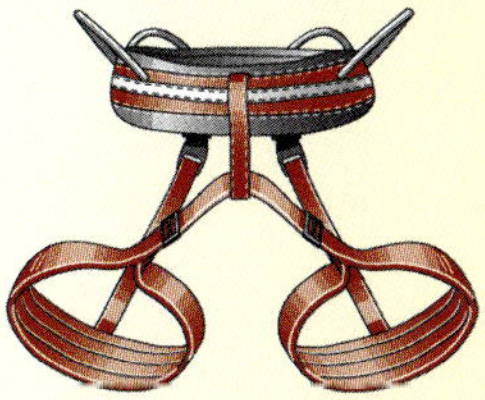

rock shoes are thin-soled and made of high-friction rubber. They are a tight fit so the climber can feel every tiny bump underfoot.

helmet
A helmet should be worn when climbing outdoors. It will protect your head from loose falling rocks.

quickdraw sets are pre-attached carabiner clip-and-sling sets used to link a rope to the fixed bolts.

bent-gate

straight-gate

carabiner
A strong steel link with a screw-gate to open it.

chalk is useful for keeping hands dry on difficult moves with only small or delicate holds.

Techniques

Middle of rope is clipped into an anchor point at top of climb.

Both ends of rope hang down to bottom of climb.

Climber clips onto one end and starts to climb.

Partner is clipped to anchor point at bottom, and takes in slack in other end of rope as climber ascends.

Climber is always protected with a tight rope, so any fall will be short.

▲ **Top-roping** is an excellent way for climbers to push themselves to their limits. Outdoor crag and cliff-climbers often use a top rope for extra protection.

The lingo

flash Climbing a route on the first attempt without falling or hanging on the rope. The climber has been given information about what moves to make on the climb.

on-sight flash A climber who has completed the entire route in the first attempt without falling and without knowing anything about the route beforehand.

pinkpoint The successful climb of a route where all the quickdraw carabiners are pre-placed. All the climber has to do for protection is to clip the rope into each carabiner.

protection Climbers give themselves protection by clipping the rope attached

WHY DO IT?

Ben is a student and avid sport climber. He is being interviewed with his flatmates while recovering from a very serious fracture.

"So is this it, Ben? Will you give up climbing now?"

"I was extremely shaken up for several weeks. I was lead-climbing when it happened. I like to take calculated risks. When I achieve a tricky move or reach the top, I get a tremendous buzz."

"You still haven't answered my question."

"No I won't give up but I'll be more moderate and err on the side of caution."

"What do your flatmates think about all this?"

"Ask them."

to their harness onto the bolts hammered into the wall.

redpoint This describes the successful climb of a route that the climber has attempted many times.

top-roping Ascending a route while clipped on to a safety rope fastened to the top of the wall. If you start to fall, the top-rope immediately checks your fall.

Some sport climbers take up the challenge of ice-climbing.

"Don't you worry about him injuring himself?"

"And you Anish. Do you feel enough is enough?"

"I'm upset that Ben has hurt himself but I admire his positive attitude. I am going to go climbing with him when he has recovered."

Michal

Anish

"Normal climbing with a rope is fairly safe. I just feel Ben pushed himself beyond his limits. Now he feels he has learnt from his experience."

"I do worry about him but this time he knew he had gone beyond his own ability. He's now decided not to take unnecessary risks."

"I do get scared for him as he's much more casual about the risks than I would be. I suppose to do it in the first place you must have that attitude."

Michal

"Would you prefer it if he didn't do it?"

Sara

"No, because then he wouldn't be Ben."

Bungee Jumping

◀ This breathtaking bungee jump is using the New Zealand system where you end up hanging upside down.

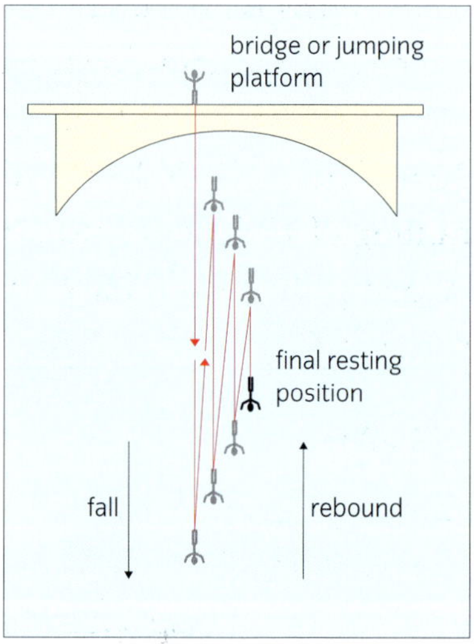

Past

According to one account, bungee jumping evolved from an incident which took place on an island in the South Pacific. The story goes that a woman, trying to run away from her husband, tied a vine round her ankle and threw herself out of a tall tree. Her husband had followed her up into the tree and leant out to catch her as she fell. He fell to his death while she was saved by the vine. The men of the village were impressed by her jump and began to hold competitions, and vine jumping became a local tradition. In 1979, a film of this unusual custom inspired the Oxford Dangerous Sports Club to try similar jumps, using rubber shock cords, which are also known as "bungee ropes". So the sport of bungee jumping was born.

▲ It all began with vine jumping!

Present

Bungee jumping is popular today all over the world.

Extreme forms of bungee jumping involve leaping from helicopters and balloons in order to extend the distance of the freefall.

In the early 1980s The British Elastic Rope Sports Association (BERSA) was founded. It has laid down a set of rules and safety regulations for bungee jumping in Great Britain. BERSA is involved in the training of club staff and it also encourages research into, and development of the sport.

Future

There are plans to arrange competitions. These will involve accuracy tests where the jumper has to grasp specific targets on the ground or in the water. A variety of acrobatic moves and tricks are also being introduced into the jumps. High-divers have proved to be brilliant at performing tricks during bungee jumps.

Equipment

In addition to a bridge, high building, or crane cage from which to fall, you will need:

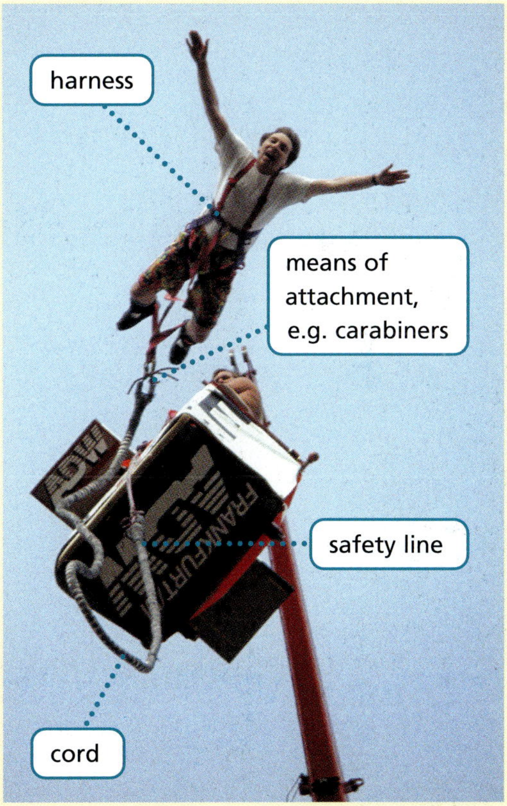

▲ Bungee jumping from a crane, using the American system with two harnesses. The chest harness helps you to turn the right way up when you have stopped bouncing.

The lingo

bungee rope Elastic rope with a core of rubber cords and a braided nylon outer casing.

freefall The downward plunge before the cord runs out and "catches", and starts to stretch and slow the fall.

rebound The upward movement which starts when the stretched cord starts to contract.

static freefall When the jumper "hovers", weightless, at the top of the bounce.

The two main systems

The European/New Zealand system uses a single rubber cord attached to a harness round the ankles, over protective padding. The thickness of the cord is selected to suit the weight of the jumper. A second safety line provides added security. This system "catches" sooner, and gives less freefall.

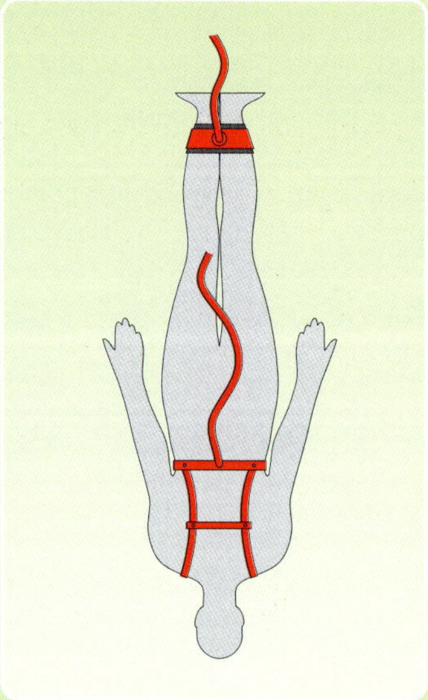

The American system uses two harnesses, one around the waist or shoulders, and one around the ankles. Extra cords are added according to the jumper's weight: one cord for each 23 kg. There are two anchor points, for extra security. This system gives more freefall and greater deceleration.

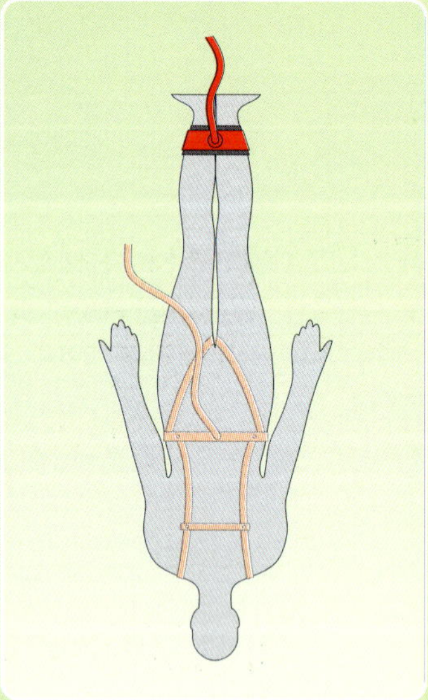

In both systems, energy is stored in the elastic cords, which stretch until they stop the freefall. Then the cords contract and propel the jumper back upwards. After a few freefalls and bounces, the jumper comes to rest.

The person's weight is written on their hand to help with double checking.

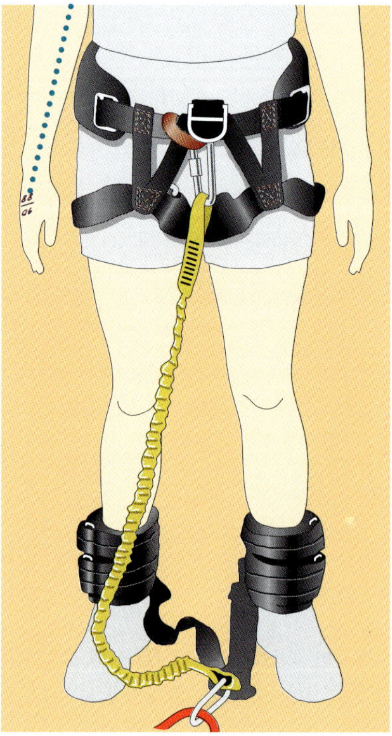

▲ Most clubs use a leg harness to take most of the weight, and a body harness or a climbing harness for back-up. The body harness also makes the ride more comfortable if you have to be hauled back up.

WHY DO IT?

"This was my first time. I thought the worst part of it would be hanging upside down at the bottom, but actually that wasn't so bad. Standing on the top before you jump, however, is another story. If I'd been alone I'd probably have chickened out."

Matthew

"Is it dangerous?"

"It's supposed to be safe. My greatest fear was that the rope would snap. I've heard of a couple of minor mishaps. A friend of mine had two very red eyes just from the blood rush due to deceleration."

"Why do you do it, Matthew?"

"I do it for the sheer thrill of it. It is just amazing and every jump is just as exciting as the first."

"Are you going to have a go?"

Laura

"No way! I like watching but you won't catch me leaping from a platform 50m above the ground. Like most extreme sports, you can get hurt if something goes wrong."

Quidditch and other Fantasy Sports

Quidditch

This is the most extreme of the dangerous sports covered in this book. Like the others, the players, gear and technique all play their part. However, for quidditch, one extra ingredient is required – that little bit of magic.

▼ In quidditch, the seeker has to catch the golden snitch.

So for those who think practice makes perfect, forget it! When it comes to quidditch, you just won't make it into the air unless you have some inherited wizardry, (even if, like Harry Potter, you don't discover it until aged eleven).

Equipment

A broomstick

Study your family tree. If wizard ancestry is discovered, visit "Quality Quidditch Supplies" in Diagon Alley for the complete range of broomsticks.

How to play

Quidditch is played in the air.

It is played on or rather above a pitch surrounded by hundreds of seats raised on stands so that people at the back can see.

At either end of the pitch are three golden poles with hoops on the end about 18 m high.

Each side has seven players:

three chasers
one keeper
one seeker
two beaters

There are four balls:

the quaffle
a large, red, football-sized ball
two bludgers
black and slightly smaller than the quaffle
Watch out – these can be dangerous!
the snitch
walnut-sized and bright gold with silver wings

The chasers throw the quaffle to each other, trying to put it through the hoops to score a goal and win ten points for their team.

The keeper flies around the hoops preventing the opposing team from scoring.

The bludgers whizz around and try to knock the players off their brooms.

The beaters protect their side from the bludgers and try to knock them towards the opposing team.

The seeker's job is to catch the golden snitch. This is difficult because the snitch is so fast, it is hard to see. The seeker has to weave in and out of all the other players and try to catch the snitch before the other team's seeker gets to it.

The game ends when the golden snitch is caught. The seeker who catches it wins 150 points for their team.

Rumour has it that the longest game lasted three months!

Flamingo croquet

Croquet is a fiercely competitive game when played by ordinary people on a lawn with metal hoops, and wooden balls and mallets. But when the Queen of Hearts invited Alice in Wonderland to play, flamingos were used as mallets, hedgehogs as balls and the playing-card gardeners had to bend themselves into hoops. If the Queen was not allowed to win, she would shriek "Off with his head".

In the story of *Alice in Wonderland,* the Queen of Hearts enjoyed an argumentative game of flamingo croquet.

Books for further reading

The Strange Adventures of the Dangerous Sports Club by Martin Lyster, published by The Do Not Press

Street Luge Survival Guide by Darren Lott, published by Gravity Publishing

Over The Edge
A regular guy's odyssey in extreme sports
by Michael Bane, published by Victor Gollancz

The Adventure Sports Directory, published by Central Books

Useful contacts

BERSA (The British Elastic Sports Association)
33a Canal Street,
Oxford
OX2 6BQ
Tel 01865 311179

(They can advise you if a bungee jumping club you may wish to join is BERSA certified for safe operation.)

SSSprint (Street Sled Sports International)
33a Canal Street
Oxford
OX2 6BQ

(They run the British Street Luge Championship and the only street luge school in the world.)

WARNING – DANGER

These sports are known as dangerous or extreme sports precisely because they can be dangerous. So if you are seriously considering taking up one of these sports, the essential things you should do are:

- Find out about proper training.
- Contact the official organization for that sport and check out that the organization itself is affiliated to a respected body with a good safety record.
- Make sure you have all the right equipment to try the sport with the minimum of risk.
- Arrange a contact number so that someone can be called if you need help of any sort.

Index